T0354018

Pupil's Book

1

Hopscotch

JENNIFER HEATH

NATIONAL
GEOGRAPHIC
L E A R N I N G

Australia · Brazil · Mexico · Singapore · United Kingdom · United States

Icons and Rubrics

Icon	English	My language
	Listen	
	Say/Read	
	Sing/Chant	
	Play	
	Point	
	Stick	
	Look/Watch	
	Colour	
	Make	
	Tick/Match/Circle/Number	
	Draw	
	Write	

Contents

Hello

You will learn:
* how to say hello and goodbye
* to talk about yourself
* the names of colours.

1 **Listen and say.** 1/2
2 **Listen and sing.** 1/3
3 **Play.**

What's your name?

Fred   Kate   Snap   Honey   Chatty

1 Listen and say. 1/4

Story corner

2 Listen, point and say.  1/5

1 Pupils learn and say the names of the characters. ⊃TB
2 Pupils listen to the dialogue, follow the story and repeat the phrases. ⊃TB

3 Listen and stick.

 1

2

3

4 5

4 Listen, chant and point.

5 Look and say.

 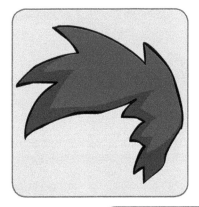 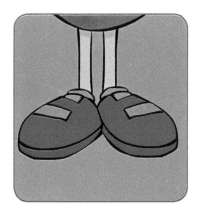

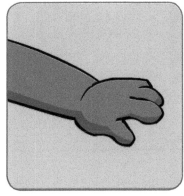 

3   Pupils listen to the recording and stick the correct stickers. ⊃TB
4   Pupils chant all together and point to the characters above.
5   Pupils look at the body parts of the main characters and say their names.

Lesson 2

Colours

red   yellow   orange   kite

1 Listen and say.

2 Listen, point and say.

1   Pupils learn and say the new words. ➲TB
2   Pupils listen to the girl speaking, point to the photo and repeat the phrases. ➲TB

3 Play.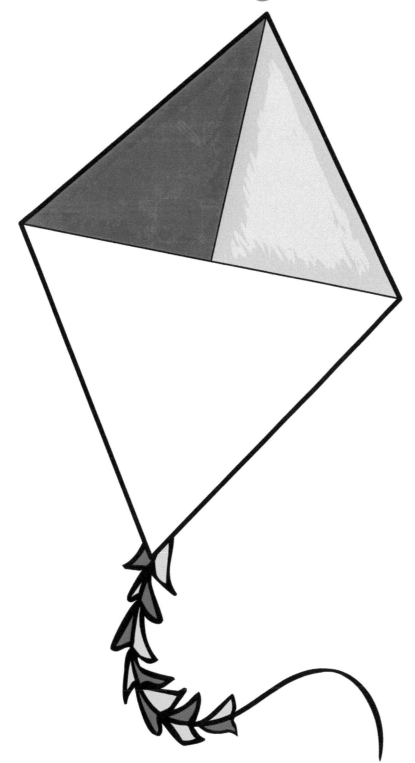

4 Colour, make and say.

5 Listen, colour and sing. 1/10

3 Pupils play the *Missing Game.* ⇒TB
4 Pupils cut out a spinning top, spin it and say what colour they can see. ⇒TB
5 Pupils listen to the song, colour the kite accordingly and sing all together.

9

Lesson 3

In the garden

blue   green   flower   tree

1 Listen and say. 1/11

2 Listen, tick and say. 1/12

1   Pupils learn and say the new words. ➲TB
2   Pupils listen to the dialogues, tick the correct photos and say the words.

3 **Listen and chant.**

4 **Listen, draw and say.**

5 **Draw, colour and say.**

   _ _ _ _ _ _   _ _ _ _ _ _   _ _ _ _ _ _

3   Pupils chant all together. ⊃TB
4   Pupils listen to the children speaking, draw the pictures and say the words.
5   Pupils complete the pattern, colour it in and say the words.

11

Wonderful world

crocodile

bear

1 Colour and say.

2 Make and say.

1 Pupils colour the parrot and name the colours. ➲TB
2 Pupils make crocodiles and role-play greetings and introductions. ➲TB

parrots

Class Project

Wild animals

Prepare pictures of wild animals living in forests and meadows. Make a poster.
Say the names of the animals and colours in English.

sky

grass

girl

boy

1 Watch, tick and say. 👀 ✏️ 💬

2 Watch, colour and say. 👀 🖌️ 💬

3 Watch and say. 👀 💬

1 Pupils watch the DVD, tick the objects they have seen and say the words.
2 Pupils watch the DVD again, colour the pictures and say the words.
3 Pupils watch the slideshows and repeat the words. ⟳TB

Review 1

1 Listen and colour.

  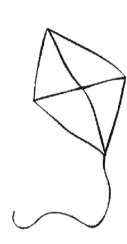

2 Listen, point and sing.

3 Say.

1 Pupils listen to the recording and colour the pictures accordingly.
2 Pupils listen to the song, point to the correct character and sing all together.
3 Pupils role-play greetings.

 **Hello!**

Check what you have already learnt.

1 I can hear, understand and point. 1/17

2 I can name the colours.

3 I can:

✳ say hello

✳ say goodbye

✳ say my name.

Pupils do the self-evaluation.

Unit 2 School

You will learn:
* names of school objects
* to ask the question: *What's this?* and to answer
* to say greetings.

1 **Listen and say.** 1/18

2 **Listen and chant.** 1/19

3 **Listen and point.** 1/20

18

Lesson 1

Thank you, Fred!

pencil   crayon   pen   rubber

1 Listen and say. 1/21

2 Listen, point and say. 1/22

Story corner

1 Pupils learn and say the new words. ⟳TB
2 Pupils listen to the dialogue, follow the story and repeat the phrases. ⟳TB

3 Match and colour.

4 Listen, point and say. 1/23

5 Listen and chant. 1/24

3   Pupils follow the lines and colour the objects accordingly.
4   Pupils listen to the recording, point to the correct objects above and repeat the phrases.
5   Pupils chant all together and hold up the correct objects.

21

Lesson 2 My classroom

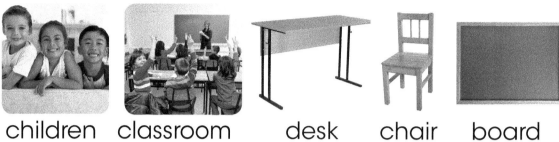

children   classroom   desk   chair   board

1 Listen and say. 1/25

2 Listen, point and say. 1/26

Lesson 2 — My classroom

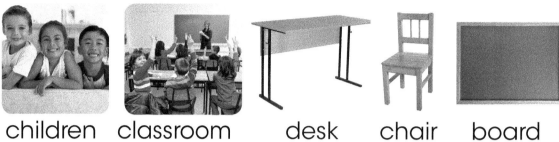

children classroom desk chair board

1 Listen and say. 1/25

2 Listen, point and say. 1/26

1 Pupils learn and say the new words. ⊃TB
2 Pupils listen to the dialogue, point to the photo and repeat the phrases.

3 Play.

4 Draw, colour and say.

5 Look and say.

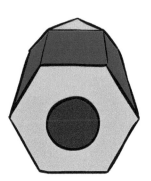

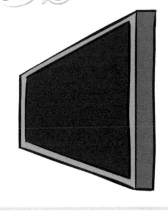

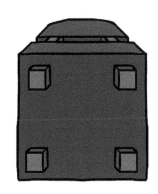

3   Pupils play the *Missing Game*.
4   Pupils complete the drawings, colour them in and name the objects.
5   Pupils look at the pictures, guess what the objects are and say the words.

My school bag

school

school bag

pencil case

book

1 Listen and say.  1/27

2 Listen and point. 1/28

3 Listen and sing.  1/29

1 Pupils learn and say the new words. ⊃TB
2 Pupils listen to the dialogue and point to the children and objects.
3 Pupils listen to the song and sing all together as the teacher holds up the correct flashcards.

4 Listen, stick and say.

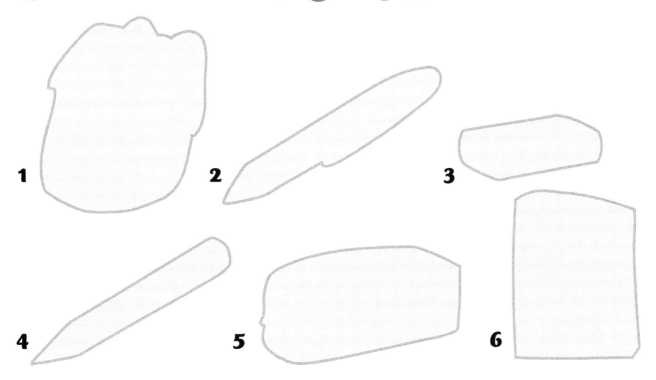

1

2

3

4

5

6

5 Draw and say.

4 Pupils listen to the recording, stick the correct stickers and name the objects.
5 Pupils draw school objects in the school bag and name them.

25

Wonderful world

floor

pupil

1 Draw and say.

2 Play.

1 Pupils draw their own classroom and name the items in their drawings.
2 Pupils play *Dominoes*. ➲TB

uniform

teacher

Class Project

Interesting places in our school

Take pictures of interesting places in your school. Display them in the classroom. Name the places and objects in English.

Our school

DVD Club

teacher

boy

school bus

girl

28

1 Watch, tick and say.

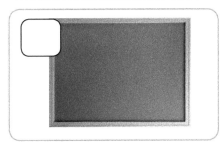
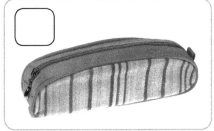

2 Watch, colour and say.

3 Watch and say.

1 Pupils watch the DVD, tick the objects they have seen and say the words.
2 Pupils watch the DVD again, colour the pictures and say the words.
3 Pupils watch the slideshows and repeat the words. ⟳TB

Review 2

1 Listen, colour and say.

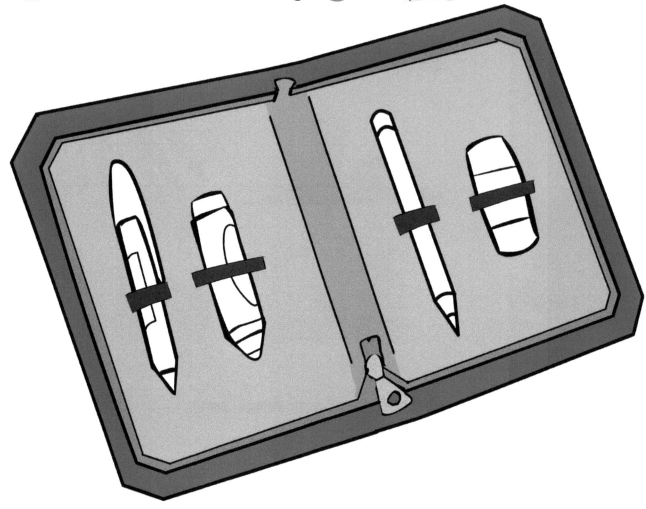

2 Listen and chant.

3 Look and say.

  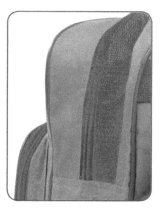 

30

1 Pupils listen to the recording, colour the objects accordingly and name them.
2 Pupils chant all together and clap their hands.
3 Pupils look at the photos, guess what the objects are and say the words.

 **School**

Check what you have already learnt.

1 I can hear, understand and point. 1/33

2 I can name school objects.

3 I can:

✻ name the places in school

✻ ask the question *What's this?* and answer

✻ say greetings.

Unit 3 Toys

You will learn:
* to name your favourite toys
* to talk about your toys.

1 **Listen, point and say.** 1/34

2 **Listen and chant.** 1/35

3 **Draw and say.**

My toy is great!

toys   car   plane   ball   drum

1 Listen and say.  1/36

Story corner

2 Listen, point and say. 1/37

1 Pupils learn and say the new words. ⊃TB
2 Pupils listen to the dialogue, follow the story and repeat the phrases. ⊃TB

3 Listen, point and say.

4 Listen and colour.

5 Listen and sing.

3 Pupils listen to the recording, point to the toys and name them. ⊃TB
4 Pupils listen to the song and colour the pictures accordingly.
5 Pupils listen to the song and sing all together as they mime playing with the toys.

A present

present

teddy bear

doll

truck

1 Listen and say. 1/41

2 Listen and point. 1/42

1 Pupils learn and say the new words. ⊃TB
2 Pupils listen to the children speaking and point to the photos.

3 **Listen and chant.** 1/43 ♫

4 **Play.**

5 **Draw and say.**

3 Pupils chant and mime playing with the toys.
4 Pupils play *Bingo*. ⊃TB
5 Pupils draw the toy they would like to have and name it.

Lesson 3

My favourite toy

guitar   trumpet   bike   train   boat

1 Listen and say. 1/44

2 Listen and stick. 1/45

1 Pupils learn and say the new words. ⊃TB
2 Pupils listen to the children speaking and stick a smiley face next to the correct photo.

3 **Listen and chant.**

4 **Play.**

5 **Look, colour and say.**

3 Pupils chant and mime playing with the toys.
4 Pupils play the *Memory Game* or *Snap*. ➲TB
5 Pupils find the hidden toys in the picture, colour and name them.

39

Wonderful world

skipping

football

1 Listen and sing. 1/47 ♪

2 Draw, colour and say.

1   Pupils listen to the song and sing all together as they dance around in a circle holding hands.
2   Pupils complete the pattern, colour it in and say the words. ➲TB

sledge

snorkelling

Class Project

Outdoor games for fun

Play a popular outdoor game.
Make a short film about it.
Name the game in English.

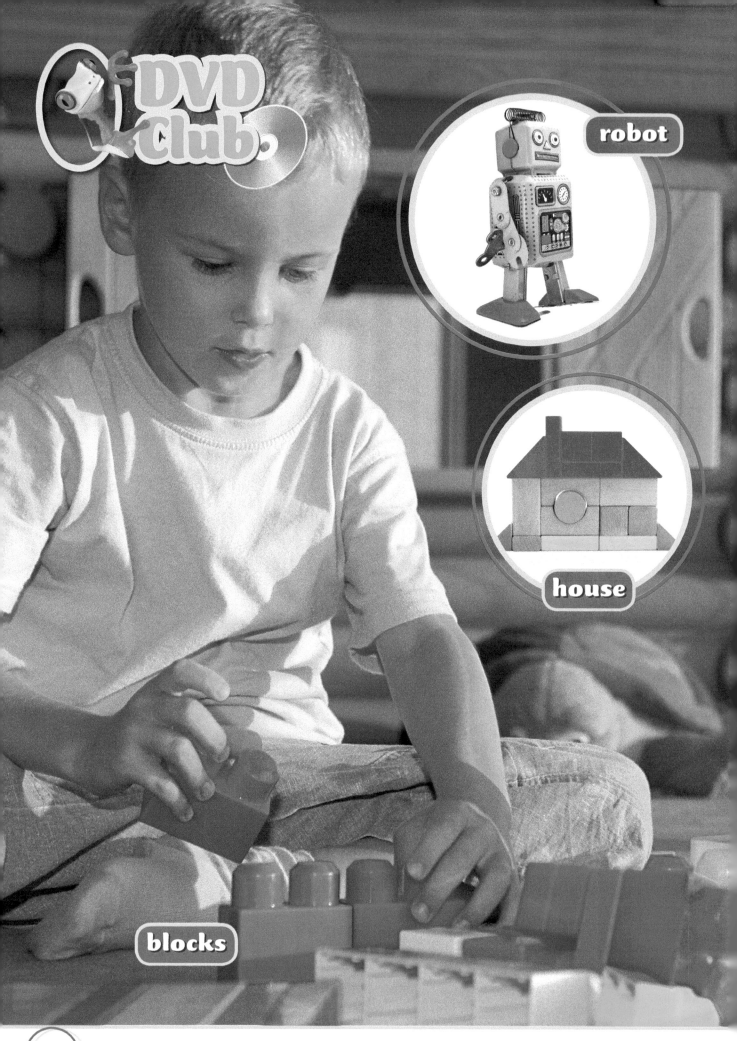

DVD Club

robot

house

blocks

1 Watch, circle and say.

1

2

3

2 Watch and play. 👀 🎲

3 Watch and say. 👀 💬

1 Pupils watch the DVD, circle the toys they have seen in the three presents and say the words.
2 Pupils watch the DVD again and mime playing with the toys in the order they see them.
3 Pupils watch the slideshows and repeat the words. ➲TB

Review 3

1 Listen and stick. 1/48

2 Play.

3 Draw, colour and say.

1 Pupils listen to the characters speaking and stick the correct stickers.
2 Pupils mime playing with a toy and other pupils guess the name of the toy.
3 Pupils finish drawing and colouring the toys on the poster and name them.

 **Toys**

Check what you have already learnt.

1 I can hear, understand and point. 1/49

2 I can name the toys.

3 I can:

* name the toys

* talk about my toys.

Unit 4 Pets

You will learn:
* to talk about your pets
* to describe the size
* to talk about things you can do.

1 Listen and say. 1/50

2 Listen and chant. 1/51 ♫

3 Draw and say.

47

I've got a parrot!

 parrot    hamster    goldfish    canary    rabbit

1 Listen and say. 1/52

2 Listen, point and say 1/53

Story corner

1   Pupils learn and say the new words. ⮐TB
2   Pupils listen to the dialogue, follow the story and repeat the phrases. ⮐TB

3 **Listen, stick and say.**

 ◯  ◯  ◯ ◯

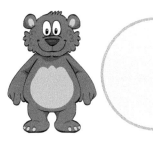 ◯  ◯

4 **Draw and say.**

3 Pupils listen to the characters speaking, stick the correct stickers and repeat the sentences.
4 Pupils draw the pet they like from this lesson and name it.

49

Big and small

cat

dog

small

big

1 Listen and say. 1/55

2 Listen, point and say. 1/56

1   Pupils learn and say the new words. ⊃TB
2   Pupils listen to the speaker, point to the photo and repeat the sentences. ⊃TB

3 **Listen and say.** 1/57

4 **Listen, point and chant.** 1/58

5 **Colour and say.**

3 Pupils listen to the animal noises and name the animals.
4 Pupils listen to the chant, point to the correct animals and chant all together.
5 Pupils complete the drawing, colour and name the animals.

51

Lesson 3
I can jump!

climb

swim

jump

run

1 Listen and say. 1/59

2 Listen, tick and say. 1/60

1 Pupils learn and say the new words. ➔TB
2 Pupils listen to the children speaking, tick the correct photos and repeat the sentences.

3 Listen, match and say.

4 Listen and sing.

5 Make and play.

3 Pupils listen to the characters speaking, match them with the actions and repeat the sentences.
4 Pupils sing all together and mime the actions.
5 Pupils make animal puppets and play with them. ➲TB

Wonderful world

monkey

insect

1 Listen and chant. 1/63

2 Colour and say.

1   Pupils chant all together and mime the actions.
2   Pupils colour the picture and describe the dogs. ⊃TB

snake

lamb

Class Project

Our favourite pets

Make models of your pets.
Prepare a class display.
Name the pets in English.

DVD Club

park

fish bowl

carrots

swing

56

1 Watch, tick and say. 👀 ✏️ 🔍

2 Watch, match and say. 👀 ✏️ 🔍

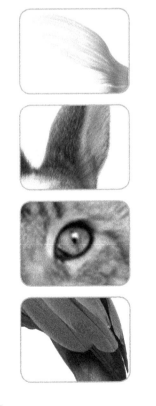

3 Watch and say. 👀 🔍

1   Pupils watch the DVD, tick the animals they have seen and say the words.
2   Pupils watch the DVD again, match the zooms with the objects and say the words.
3   Pupils watch the slideshows and repeat the words. ⤷TB

57

Review 4

1 Listen, tick and say. 1/64

2 Draw and say.

3 Play.

1 Pupils listen to the recording, tick the correct actions and repeat the sentences.
2 Pupils draw along the lines and say what the animals can do.
3 Pupils play *Simon Says.* ↪TB

 **Pets**

Check what you have already learnt.

1 I can hear, understand and point. 1/65

2 I can name the pets.

3 I can:

* talk about my pets

* describe the size

* talk about what I can do.

My family

You will learn:
* to talk about how you feel and ask about others
* to introduce your relatives
* to talk about your home.

1 **Listen and point.** 2/1

2 **Listen and say.** 2/2

3 **Listen and chant.** 2/3

This is my brother.

brother sister   baby   friends

1 Listen and say. 2/4

Story corner

2 Listen, point and say. 2/5

1 Pupils learn and say the new words. ⊃TB
2 Pupils listen to the dialogue, follow the story and repeat the sentences. ⊃TB

3 **Listen and sing.**

4 **Write, match and read.**

brother   sister

baby   friend

5 **Colour and say.**

3 Pupils listen to the song and sing it all together. ⊃TB
4 Pupils trace over the words, match them to the characters and read them.
5 Pupils colour the characters and say who is in the picture.

63

Mummy and daddy

family   mummy daddy   grandma grandpa

1 **Listen and say.**

2 **Listen, point and say.**

1   Pupils learn and say the new words. ⊃TB
2   Pupils listen to the boy speaking, point to the people and repeat the sentences.

3 Listen and stick. 2/9

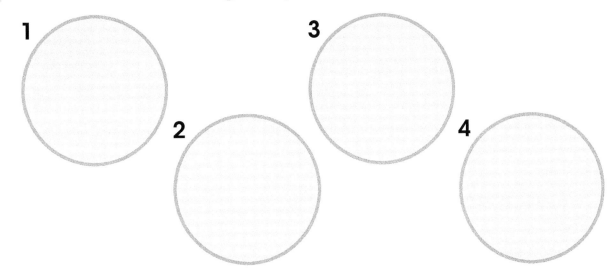

1

2

3

4

4 Listen and chant. 2/10 ♪

5 Draw and say.

3   Pupils listen to the girl speaking and stick the correct stickers.
4   Pupils chant all together.
5   Pupils draw the family member of their choice and say who it is.

65

My house

house   kitchen   bathroom   living room   bedroom

1 Listen and say. 2/11

2 Look and match.

3 Listen and say. 2/12

1   Pupils learn and say the new words. ⊃TB
2   Pupils match the family members to the rooms.
3   Pupils listen to the boy speaking, check their answers and then repeat the sentences.

4 Look and say.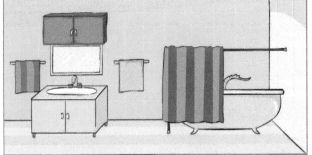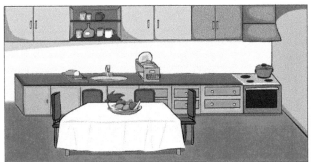

5 Colour and say.

6 Make and play.

4   Pupils find the hidden characters and say who is in which room.
5   Pupils colour the pictures and say where the family members are.
6   Pupils make family puppets and play with them. ◯TB

67

Wonderful world

hut

igloo

1 Draw and say.

2 Play.

1 Pupils draw their house or a house of their dreams and name the rooms.
2 Pupils play *Snap*. ➲TB

tepee

yurt

Class Project

Our homes

Make models of your homes.
Use different materials and
techniques.
Prepare a class display.
Describe the models in
English.

DVD Club

town

garden

hall

stairs

70

1 Watch, tick and say.

2 Watch, colour and say.

3 Watch and say.

1 Pupils watch the DVD, tick the people or objects they have seen and say the words.
2 Pupils watch the DVD again, colour the picture and say the words.
3 Pupils watch the slideshows and repeat the words. ⊃TB

Review 5

1 Colour and say.

2 Match and say.

3 Listen and sing.  2/13

1 Pupils colour the picture, point to the people and name them.
2 Pupils follow the lines and say where the family members are. ⟳TB
3 Pupils listen to the song and sing it all together.

I can! My family

Check what you have already learnt.

1 I can hear, understand and point. 2/14

2 I can name my relatives.

3 I can:

* ✳ talk about how I feel and ask about others

* ✳ introduce a friend and members of my family

* ✳ talk about my home.

My body

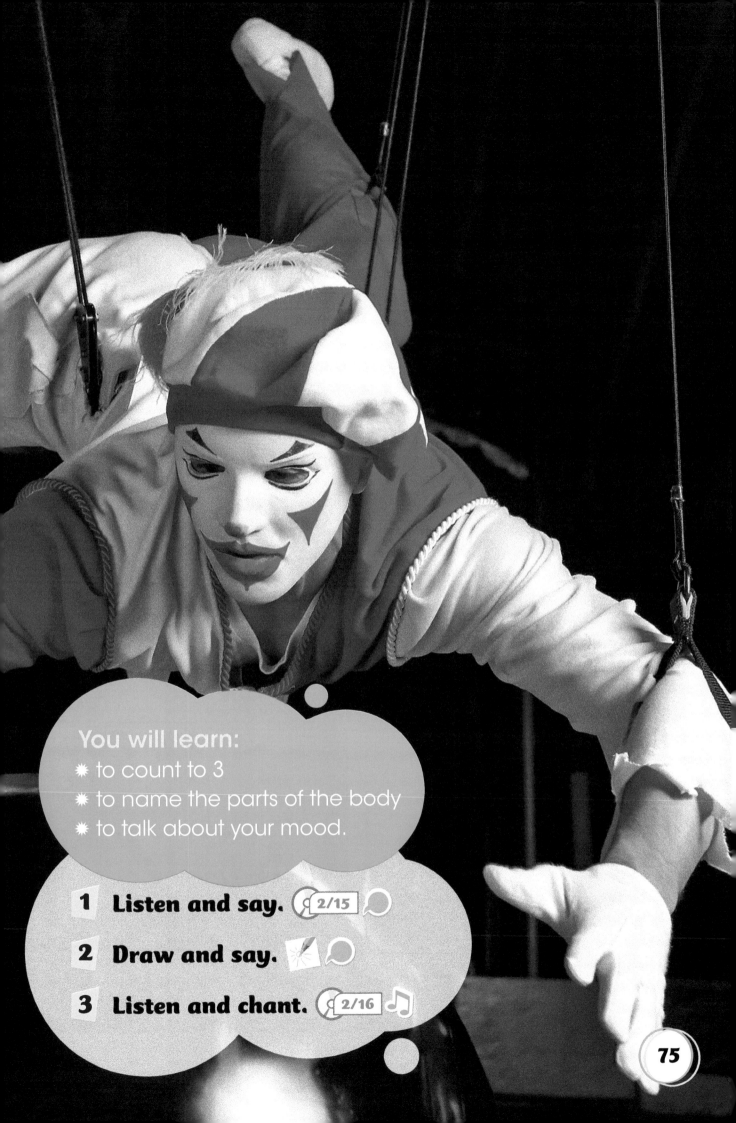

You will learn:
* to count to 3
* to name the parts of the body
* to talk about your mood.

1 Listen and say. 2/15

2 Draw and say.

3 Listen and chant. 2/16

75

Lesson 1 — Hands up!

hands   feet   one   two   three

1 Listen and say. 2/17

Story corner

2 Listen, point and say. 2/18

1   Pupils learn and say the new words. ➲TB
2   Pupils listen to the dialogue, follow the story and repeat the sentences. ➲TB

3 **Listen, colour and say.**

4 **Listen and sing.**

5 **Listen, point and say.**

3 Pupils listen to the recording, colour the numbers and repeat the sentences.
4 Pupils sing all together and show their hands and feet.
5 Pupils listen to the recording, point to the correct part of the picture and repeat the sentences.

77

I've got two eyes.

eyes   ears   mouth   nose

1 Listen and say. ⟨2/22⟩ 🔍

2 Listen, point and chant. ⟨2/23⟩ ✋ 🎵

1 Pupils learn and say the new words. ⟳TB
2 Pupils listen to the boy chanting, point to the photo and chant all together.

3 **Listen and number.** 2/24

4 **Make and say.**

5 **Write and read.**

ears   eyes   nose   mouth

3   Pupils listen to the robots speaking and number the pictures accordingly.
4   Pupils make fun masks and describe them. ➲TB
5   Pupils trace over the words and say them.

I'm happy!

leg   tummy   arm

happy   sad

1 Listen and say. 2/25

2 Listen, number and say. 2/26

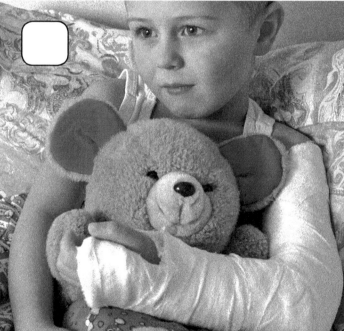

1   Pupils learn and say the new words. ⊃TB
2   Pupils listen to the children speaking, number the photos in the correct order and repeat the sentences.

3 Listen, colour and say.  2/27

4 Listen and sing. 2/28

5 Play.

3   Pupils listen to the boy speaking and colour the teddy bear accordingly.
4   Pupils sing all together and point to the picture above.
5   Pupils play the *Guessing Game.* ⤳TB

Wonderful world

wing

1 Listen and play.

2 Draw and say.

1 Pupils listen to the music and move around the classroom. ➲TB
2 Pupils draw pictures of totem poles and describe them. ➲TB

teeth

head

Class Project

Monsters

Make models of different funny monsters. Use different materials and techniques. Prepare a class display. Name the parts of the monsters' bodies in English.

DVD Club

head

hair

snowman

black

1 Watch, circle and read.

head   eyes   ears   mouth

nose   (tummy)   (arms)

legs   feet   hair

2 Watch, colour and say.

3 Watch and say.

1 Pupils watch the DVD, circle the words with appropriate colours and read them.
2 Pupils watch the DVD again, colour the picture and say the words.
3 Pupils watch the slideshows and repeat the words. ⟳TB

85

Review

1 **Listen and draw.**

2 **Write, stick and read.**

eye

hands

ear

feet

3 **Play.**

1 Pupils listen to the monster speaking and complete the drawing.
2 Pupils trace over the words, stick the correct stickers and read the words.
3 Pupils play *Simon Says*.

 **My body**

Check what you have already learnt.

1 I can hear, understand and point.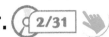

2 I can name the parts of the body.

   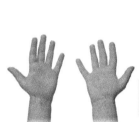 

3 I can:

* count to 3

* decide if something is big or small

* talk about my mood.

Unit 7 The weather

You will learn:
* ❋ to talk about the weather
* ❋ to count to 6
* ❋ to talk about clothes.

1 Listen and say. 2/32

2 Listen and chant. 2/33

3 Listen and play. 2/34

I like sun!

sun

rain

wind

snow

1 Listen and say.

Story corner

2 Listen, point and say.

1 Pupils learn and say the new words. ➾TB
2 Pupils listen to the dialogue, follow the story and repeat the sentences. ➾TB

3 **Listen and sing.**  2/37 ♪

4 **Stick and say.**

1

2

3

4

5 **Write, read and match.**

sun   rain   wind   snow

3 Pupils sing all together.
4 Pupils stick the correct stickers and say the words.
5 Pupils trace over the words, read them and match them to the correct pictures above.

Lesson 2

It's cold!

hot   cold   **4** four   **5** five   **6** six

1 Listen and say. (2/38)

2 Listen, point and say. (2/39)

92

1 Pupils learn and say the new words. ➲TB
2 Pupils listen to the children speaking, point to the photos and repeat the sentences.

3 **Listen and chant.**

4 **Colour and say.**

5 **Listen and number.**

3 Pupils chant all together and clap their hands. ➲TB
4 Pupils colour the numbers and say the phrases. ➲TB
5 Pupils listen to the recording and number the pictures accordingly.

Lesson 3 Clothes

shorts   T-shirt   skirt   hat   sweater   jeans

1 Listen and say. 2/42

2 Listen, number and say. 2/43

1   Pupils learn and say the new words. ⟳TB
2   Pupils listen to the children speaking, number the people in the photos from 1 to 6 and repeat the sentences.

3 Listen, colour and say.

4 Play.

Wonderful world

lightning

icicles

1 Listen and sing. (2/45) ♪

2 Make and say. ✂ ●

1   Pupils sing all together.
2   Pupils make a weather mobile and say appropriate weather words. ⊃TB

rainbow

Class Project

Spring in our neighbourhood

Look for the first signs of spring in your neighbourhood. Make a poster about this trip. Use different materials and techniques. Name the objects in the poster in English.

Pupils do a class project. ➲TB

DVD Club

clouds

sledge

rainbow

jacket

boots

98

umbrella

1 **Watch and number.**

2 **Watch, colour and say.**

3 **Watch and say.**

1   Pupils watch the DVD and number the photos in the order they have seen them.
2   Pupils watch the DVD again, colour the pictures and say the words.
3   Pupils watch the slideshows and repeat the words. ➲TB

Review 7

1 Match and say. ✏️ 💬

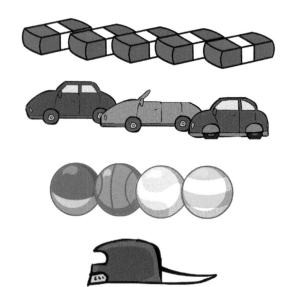

2 Listen and match. 🎧 2/46 ✏️

3 Listen and chant. 🎧 2/47 🎵

100

1   Pupils match the numbers with the correct pictures and say how many objects there are.
2   Pupils listen to the characters speaking and match them to the weather they like.
3   Pupils listen and chant all together. ⟳TB

I can! The weather

Check what you have already learnt.

---

1 I can hear, understand and point.

   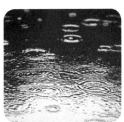 

---

2 I can name the clothes.

---

3 I can:

✱ talk about the weather

✱ count to 6

✱ talk about my clothes.

Unit

8

Food

You will learn:
* to name the food
* to talk about your favourite food
* to count to 10.

1 **Listen and say.** (2/49)

2 **Listen and sing.** (2/50)

3 **Draw, colour and say.**

I like oranges!

orange

apple

banana

pear

1 Listen and say. 2/51

Story corner

2 Listen, point and say. 2/52

1 Pupils learn and say the new words. ⊃TB
2 Pupils listen to the dialogue, follow the story and repeat the sentences. ⊃TB

3 Listen and sing. (2/53) ♪

4 Stick and say.

5 Write, read and match.

orange   apple   banana   pear

3   Pupils sing all together. ➪TB
4   Pupils stick the stickers in the baskets and say what they like and what they don't like.
5   Pupils trace over the words, read them and match them to the correct stickers.

105

Super sandwiches

sandwich   cheese   tomato   onion   meat

1 Listen and say. 2/54

2 Listen, point and say. 2/55

1 Pupils learn and say the new words. ⟳TB
2 Pupils listen to the children speaking, point to the photo and repeat the sentences.

3 Write, read and match.

meat   sandwich   onion

tomato   cheese

4 Listen and draw. 2/56

5 Listen and chant. 2/57

3   Pupils trace over the words, read them and then match them to the pictures.
4   Pupils listen to the characters speaking and draw happy or sad faces.
5   Pupils chant all together. ➲TB

Party time!

cake   seven   eight   nine   ten

1 **Listen and say.** `2/58`

2 **Listen, point and say.** `2/59`

1   Pupils learn and say the new words. ⊃TB
2   Pupils listen to the children speaking, point to the correct photos and repeat the sentences.

3 **Listen, circle and say.**

1 7 / 8   2 9 / 6   3 1 / 10

4 5 / 3   5 7 / 8   6 2 / 6

4 **Listen and chant.** 2/61 ♫

5 **Listen and draw.** 2/62

3   Pupils listen to the children speaking, circle the correct numbers and repeat the sentences.
4   Pupils chant all together.
5   Pupils listen to the characters speaking and draw the correct number of candles on the cakes. ➲TB

109

Wonderful world

sushi

1 Play.

2 Draw and say.

1   Pupils play the *Guessing Game*. ⊃TB
2   Pupils draw their favourite food and name it. ⊃TB

dumplings

noodles

Class Project

Fruit salad

Make a fruit salad.
Invite your friends and
relatives.
Take pictures.
Name the fruit in the salad
in English.

DVD Club

pizza

bread

fruit

strawberries

112

1 Watch, circle and say.

7 **8** 9 **10**

8 **9** 10

7 8 9 **10**

2 Watch, tick and say.

pizza ☐ banana ☐ tomatoes ☐

sandwich ☐ orange juice ☐ fruit ☐

apple ☐ orange ☐ bread ☐

pear ☐ cake ☐ cheese ☐

3 Colour and say.

4 Watch and say.

orange juice

1 Pupils watch the DVD, circle the children's age and say the words.
2 Pupils watch the DVD, tick the words they have heard and read them.
3 Pupils colour the pictures and say the words.
4 Pupils watch the slideshows and repeat the words. ⊃TB

113

Review 8

1 **Look, colour and say.**

2 **Listen, draw and say.** 2/63

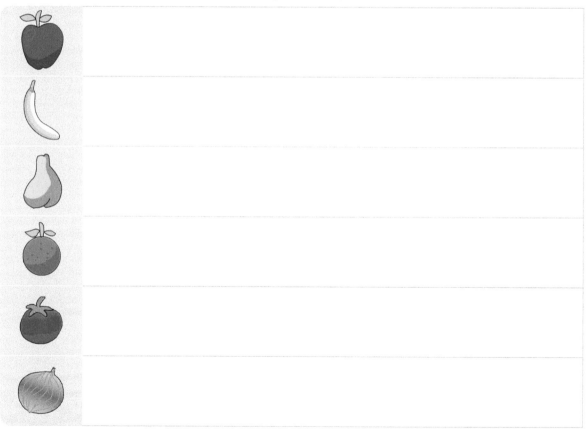

3 **Listen and chant.** 2/64

1 Pupils find the hidden numbers, colour them and say the words.
2 Pupils listen to the recording, draw the correct number of food items and repeat the phrases.
3 Pupils chant all together and clap their hands.

 **Food**

Check what you have already learnt.

1 I can hear, understand and point. 2/65

2 I can name different types of food.

3 I can:

* count to 10

* talk about my favourite food

* talk about age.

 **Celebrations** **Christmas**

Christmas tree   Father Christmas   star   lights

1 Listen and say.

2 Listen, point and say.

3 Colour, make and say.

4 Listen and sing.

(116)

1   Pupils learn and say the new words. ➜TB
2   Pupils listen to the boy speaking, point to the photos and repeat the phrases.
3   Pupils cut out the star, colour it in and say what they have got. ➜TB
4   Pupils sing a carol all together.

Easter

Easter egg

basket

Easter bunny

chick

1 Listen and say. 2/69

2 Listen, point and say. 2/70

3 Colour, make and say.

4 Listen and sing. 2/71

1 Pupils learn and say the new words. ⊃TB
2 Pupils listen to the girl speaking, point to the photo and repeat the sentences.
3 Pupils make an Easter basket, place the eggs, the chick and the bunny inside and say what they have got. ⊃TB
4 Pupils sing an Easter song all together.

Goldilocks and the Three Bears

daddy bear

mummy bear

1 Listen and say. 2/72

2 Listen, point and say. 2/73

1 Pupils learn and say the new words. ⊃TB
2 Pupils listen to the dialogue, follow the story and repeat the phrases.

baby bear

Goldilocks

porridge

3 **Play.**

NATIONAL
GEOGRAPHIC
L E A R N I N G

Hopscotch Pupil's Book 1

Jennifer Heath

Publisher: Gavin McLean

Editorial Manager: Claire Merchant

Project Manager: Dorothy Robertson

Editor: Carole Hughes

Head of Production: Celia Jones

Art Director cover: Alex von Dallwitz

Senior Designer cover: Cari Wynkoop

Compositor: MPS Limited

Audio Producer: Liz Hammond

Acknowledgements:

Audio recorded at Motivation Sound Studios and GFS-PRO Studio.

Music composed by Evdoxia Banani and Vagelis Markontonis

Production at GFS-PRO Studio by George Flamouridis

For product information and technology assistance, contact us at
Cengage Learning Customer & Sales Support, cengage.com/contact

For permission to use material from this text or product,
submit all requests online at **cengage.com/permissions**
Further permissions questions can be emailed to
permissionrequest@cengage.com

ISBN: 978-1-4080-9796-0

National Geographic Learning
Cheriton House, North Way, Andover, Hampshire, SP10 5BE
United Kingdom

National Geographic Learning, a Cengage Learning Company, has a mission to bring the world to the classroom and the classroom to life. With our English language programs, students learn about their world by experiencing it. Through our partnerships with National Geographic and TED Talks, they develop the language and skills they need to be successful global citizens and leaders.

Locate your local office at **international.cengage.com/region**

Visit National Geographic Learning online at **NGL.Cengage.com/ELT**
Visit our corporate website at **www.cengage.com**

Cover Photo: Mikronan6/Moment/Getty Images

Shutterstock:
2, 3, 8, 9, 10, 11, 14, 15, 16, 17, 20, 21, 22, 23, 24, 25, 26 bkgd, 27 bm, bl, br, 28, 29, 30, 31, 34, 36 tl, tml, tmr, tr, ml, bl, bm, br, 37, 38, 39, 40, 41, 42, 43, 44, 45, 46-47, 48, 49, 50, 51, 52, 54 b, 55 t, bl, bm, br, 56, 57, 58, 59, 62, 63, 64, 65, 66, 68, 69, 70, 71 tl, tm, m, mr, b, 72, 73, 74-75, 76, 77, 78 tl, tml, tmr,tr, 79, 80, 81, 82, 83, 84, 85, 86, 87, 88-89, 90, 92, 94, 96 bkgd, t, 97, 98, 99 tl, tmr, bl, br, bmr, 100, 101, 102-103, 104, 106 tl, tml, tm, tmr, tr, 108, 109, 110 b, 111 b, 112, 113 mb, bl, br, 114, 115, 116, 117 tl, tml, tmr, tr, br, Stickers Unit 3-6

National Geographic:
pp 4-5 (Frans Lanting/National Geographic Creative), 12 t (Frans Lanting/National Geographic Creative), 12 b (Joel Sartore/National Geographic Creative), 18-19 (XPacifica/National Geographic Creative), 26 t (Lynn Johnson/National Geographic Creative), 26 b (Skip Brown/National Geographic Creative), 27 t (Annie Griffiths Belt/National Geographic Creative), 27 tm (Karewn Kasmauski/National Geographic Creative), 32-33 (Pete Ryan/National Geographic Creative), 54 t (Frans Lanting/National Geographic Creative), 60-61 (Mattias Klum/National Geographic Creative), 78 b (John Burcham/National Geographic Creative), 96 b (John Burcham/National Geographic Creative), 111 t (Frank And Helen Schreider/National Geographic Creative),

Others:
13 (Roy Toft/Getty Images), 36 mr (Yuri Arcurs/Agefotostock), 55 mr (Glowimages/Getty Images), 71 tr (ClassicStock/Alamy), 71 ml (Zoonar GmbH/Alamy), 99 tr (Phoebe Dunn/Stock Connection Blue/Alamy), 99 tml (Fcscafeine/iStockphoto), 99 bml (Vnosokin/iStockphoto), 106 b (Wenn Ltd/Stock Photo/Alamy), 110 (XPacifica/The Image Bank/Getty Images), 113 tm (Kate Sept2004/iStockphoto), 113 m (Polka Dot Images/Jupiterimages), 117 m (Stephen St. John/Getty Images), Stickers: Unit 3 (John Leaver/Dreamstime), Unit 4 (GlobalP/iStockphoto), Unit 5 Man (Yuri/iStockphoto)

Printed in the United Kingdom by Ashford Colour Press Ltd.
Print Number: 03   Print Year: 2024

MIX
Paper | Supporting
responsible forestry
FSC® C011748